סיפור המספרים

THE NUMBER STORY

SMALL BOOK ONE

ENGLISH - HEBREW

Numbers Teach Children Their Number Names

written and illustrated by

MISS ANNA

Early Reader Edition of *The Number Story 1*
Bronze Medal Winner, 2016 Wishing Shelf Book Award

LUMPY PUBLISHING

Library of Congress Control Number: 2018902040

Names: Miss Anna, author.
Title: Number story : numbers teach children their number names / Miss Anna.
Description: Portland, OR: Lumpy Publishing, 2018.
Identifiers: ISBN 978-1-945977-30-5 | LCCN 2018902040
Summary: The pictures and rhymes present stories which introduce numbers 0-10.
Subjects: LCSH Numeration—English--Hebrew--Pictorial works--Juvenile literature. | BISAC JUVENILE NONFICTION /
Languages: English--Hebrew
Classification: LCC QA141.3 .M57 2018 | DDC 513—dc23

Publisher: Lumpy Publishing
Website: www.missannabooks.com
Email: missanna@missannabooks.com

Paperback: ISBN 978-1-945977-30-5
Printed in the U.S.A.   1 3 5 7 9 10 8 6 4 2

רוצים ללמוד את שמות המספרים שלנו?

It is very easy and a lot of fun!

זה קל מאוד והרבה כיף!

Say-along our little jingle

לשיר אתנו את הסיפור הקטן שלנו!

starting from Number One!

נתחיל ממספר אחד!

1

ONE looks like my one finger.

א אחד

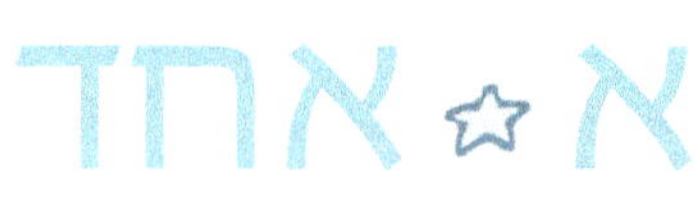

אחד נראה כמו אצבע אחת שלי.

ONE!
אחד!

2

TWO   trails a tail.

בשתים

שתיים אחריו זנב.

A TAIL!
זנב!

3

THREE has bumps.

שלוש ג

שלוש כמו גבעה.

תסתכל על הגבעות הירוקות!

4

FOUR carries a sail.

ארבע ✦ ד

.לארבע יש מפרש

A SAIL!
מפרש!

5

FIVE   is a racing track.

ה ★ חמש

★ חמש הוא מסלול המרוצים.

VROOM
¡Brrrrr!

6

SIX   curves like a snail.

שש ו

שש עקומה כמו שבלול.

A SNAIL!

שבלול!

7

OUCH!
!אאוץ
BE CAREFUL! IT'S SHARP!
!הזהר! היא חדה

8

EIGHT is rollercoaster rails.

ח • שמונה

שמונה היא מסילת רכבת הרים.

יש!
YIPPEE!

9

NINE   is a bubble on a stick.

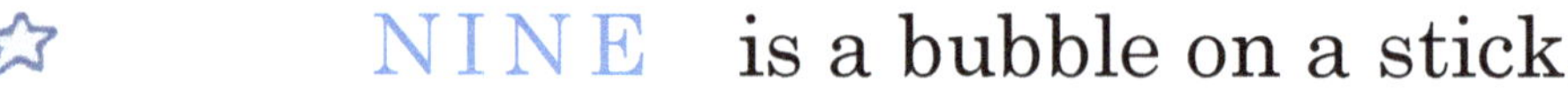

ט תשע

תשע היא בועה על מקל.

A BUBBLE! בועה !

10

TEN is an eye of a whale.

י עשר

עשר היא עין אחת של לווייתן.

WINK!
קריצה!
HELLO! שלום!

And

ו

O

ZERO   is an empty pail.

אפס

אפס הוא דלי ריק.

IT'S EMPTY!
הוא ריק!

Thank you for playing with us today.

We had a lot of fun too!

תודה ששיחקת אתנו היום.

גם לנו היה כיף!

We are your Number friends,
Zero to Ten,
Who will be here for you~

אנחנו החברים שלכם
מאפס עד עשר.
אנחנו תמיד נהיה כאן בשבילכם.

Bye-bye now!
See you again soon.

ביי ביי עכשיו!
נתראה שוב בקרוב!

The Numbers are *SINGING* too!

To sing-a-long, look for Miss Anna Number Story
at your favorite music store like iTUNES.

MP3

Numbers 0-10
IDENTIFYING & COUNTING

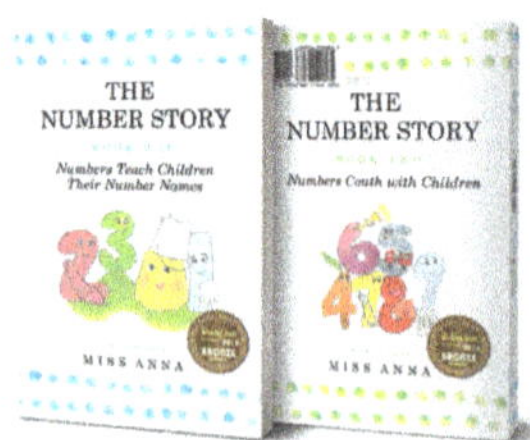

Number Story 1 & 2

isbn: 978-0-996216-48-7

Numbers 11-20 & Ordinals
first, second, third...

Number Story 3 & 4

isbn: 978-1-945977-01-5

Numbers 0-100 & Place Values
ones, tens, hundreds...

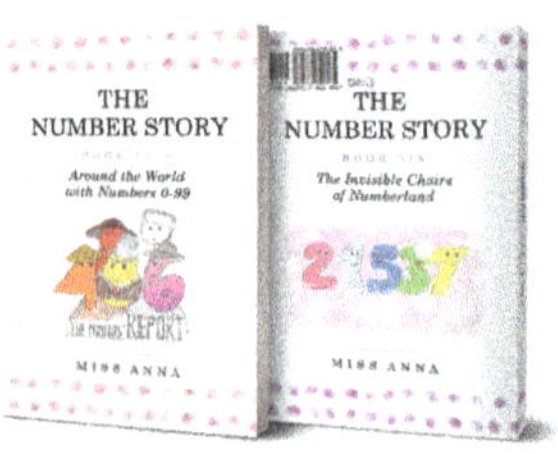

Number Story 5 & 6

isbn: 978-1-945977-06-0

About Clocks & Telling Time
hours, minutes, seconds

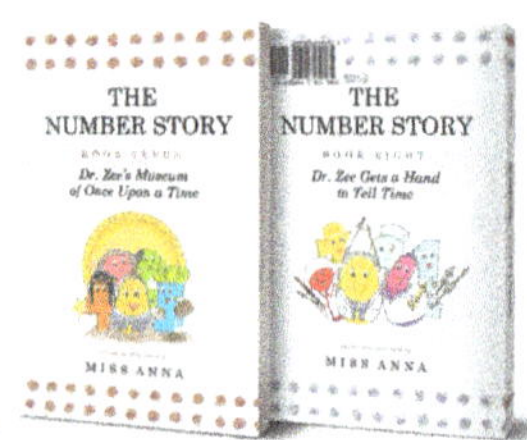

Number Story 7 & 8

isbn: 978-1-949320-40-4

For more Miss Anna books to love,
visit us at

www.missannabooks.com

Numbers are working hard all over the world!
Come Travel the World with Us!